DEEP LEARNING AND

ARTIFICIAL INTELLIGENCE

Author: John Slavio

TABLE OF CONTENTS

DISCLAIMER

ABOUT THE AUTHOR

John Slavio is a programmer who is passionate about the reach of the internet and the interaction of the internet with daily devices. He has automated several home devices to make them 'smart' and connect them to high speed internet. His passions involve computer security, iOT, hardware programming and blogging. Below is a list of his books:

John Slavio Special

INTRODUCTION

Welcome to this book on Deep Learning and Neural Networks. We're going to be diving into what neural networks are, what the current neural networks out there do, with an API. Once we go over how everything works and how each of these new technologies work, we will also go over the many different applications that can be applied to general life and business due to the creation of neural networks. Now I want you to realize that neural networks are not a complicated topic but it may feel like a complicated topic.

There have been a lot of news stories about how there are going to be self-driving cars, machines that make their own products, and many other different applications of neural networks that make it sound like a vastly complicated machine. However, the tool of the neural network is a very simple tool. When you hear about the applications that are being created that utilize neural networks, you are actually hearing about the amount of work that went behind making a neural network do something that's complicated but not a complicated neural network. Neural networks are extremely easy to understand as you will find throughout this book but the problem is that people have made them look complicated. Therefore, let's go ahead and demystify this subject so that you can get into the field of neural networks yourself and have some fun.

WHAT ARE NEURAL NETWORKS?

A neural network is a network of neurons that are either simulated or un-simulated. The neural networks that you hear about in the news and in the technology magazines are neural networks that are built out of machines and code but the original idea comes from the biological neural networks that we have within our own systems. The neural network is a very efficient and yet very simplistic form of logical progression that allows for extreme calculations to solve complex problems.

Types of Neural Networks

There are many different forms of a neural network due to the many different ways that a neural network could be used. For instance, the same type of neural network that would be used to recognize things inside of an image is very different from the neural network that is best used for translating language or spoken words that people use on a daily basis. You could think of the image needing a neural network that can recognize the different color spectrums inside of the photograph while, on the other hand, the language detection neural network would need to constantly change what it thinks that the context of the words you are using is and this is because language changes over time and is somewhat fluid, which means that you need to be able to change the definition of the word as people move forward. A voice recognition program, on the other hand, needs to be able to constantly change due to the constantly changing nature of language and the spoken word itself. A great example of this is Google Voice, which is a software that Google developed many years ago and that was very horrible in the beginning. However, given some time and some heavy amounts of practice, Google has managed to transform such a horrible software into one of the best speech recognition software on the planet that has the highest amount of accuracy when it comes to recognizing the speech patterns that we have. It also is able to predict the next word in the sentence using the words in the current sentence on context.

Applications

Neural networks are not created for pure convenience but due to the potential usefulness that neural networks could provide. Since we can't put ourselves into machines, being able to put our own abilities inside of machines would be extremely useful under certain circumstances. Image recognition would be able to tell whether we have a criminal inside of an airport, speech recognition would be able to detect whether someone was currently in a very stressful situation, there are neural networks that provide services to lawyers who can't simply look up the entire database that lawyers have access to in order to find that one, very specific, case that someone worked on many years ago that proves or disproves a constitutional action. The list goes on and on for the different types of applications that neural networks can provide when it comes to utilizing it in our everyday lives. It doesn't stop at being useful for civilians either because it is also useful for businesses when it comes to predicting future markets, when it comes to trying to make new logos or graphical designs, and even auto building websites from scratch that have been thoroughly tested for security problems. These neural networks could easily replace almost every job on the planet, which is another thing that a lot of the greater minds on this planet have begun to see and even fear. After all, if the robots can do all the jobs on the planet then why in the world are we needed? Don't worry, we're still far from the day where neural networks have the ability of self-consciousness, but scientists say that the day will come and once the neural network is self-conscious, it will be able to build new neural networks at far greater speeds than we currently have.

The Components of a Neural Network

There are three components that make up a neural network and these represent the components that go inside of us. You have an input of information, a thing that does something in the middle, and the output that is the result. If this sounds a lot like your standard program, you are correct in this assumption because neural networks are not that complicated and their creation is a rather clever application of how a program works. Inside of a normal human brain, you have a neuron, an axon, and we are both the place of input and output. Inside of a neural network, you have an input, you have a neuron, and then where you put the output is really what determines what type of machine you have in terms of neural networking.

BIOLOGICAL NEURAL NETWORK

The original concept for how our more common digital neural networks work come from the biological networks that we have within our own brains. Scientists believed that this would be one of the only solutions when it came to build a complex machine that could solve problems. This is due to the simplistic nature of the neural network that we have in our heads. You see, when we have a thought, we have electricity running through our neurons. Neurons are corner pieces of membranes within our brains that serve as an input and output switch. Neurons are connected through thin membrane wires that allow electrical pathways to traverse in between them. Unlike the more silicon friendly neural networks that we know of, neural networks in our brains are connected by multiple neurons going to and from them. A neural node can have anywhere from two to even eight different connections and maybe more that allow for electricity to go through and out of that neural node. In some instances, we have managed to get to the point where we are able to replicate such an advanced neural node but, for the most part, we stick with the input

14

and output of two connections in the long run. This is because of how simplistic the nature behind neural nodes is. A neural node is allowed to have some bias, some electrical pathway, and to produce a result that leads to another neural node. These neurons collectively form our brains, which is how it thinks. The simplistic part of it is that there are only about four components in total that make up a neuron node network. You have the neuron node, the connections, the input to the neural node, and the network itself. Due to the simplicity of this network, you can form several complex and ever scaling networks to solve problems that are far more complex than the network that you're creating. By replicating the network, scientists have begun to give us the ability to solve complex problems with simplistic solutions. After all, we are able to create a neural network on a Raspberry Pi processor that is sufficient enough to run some of the more small-scale applications that neural networks can provide. A Raspberry Pi is around $30 to $40, which means that we can basically give access to neural networks to nearly everyone who is capable of owning a computer.

The Problem

The problem that we have with biological neural networks is that biological neural networks are not completely understood yet. Sure, we understand their general function and even some of the deeper level components that come with the neuron network that we have in our brain. The problem is that we don't fully understand how it actually works and so we're making an educated guessing game when it comes to figuring out how neurons really work. For instance, there are several different projects that try to map out how neurons can actually identify objects as the same objects as they identified before. They do this by planting a whole bunch of electrodes on top of the skull so that they can map the frequency that occurs when an object is placed in front of them. Therefore, we are basing the neural network that we're utilizing in our machine on an incomplete knowledge of networks inside of our heads. This means that there are several clever ways of devising neural networks to do specific tasks but there is no one best way when it comes to neural networking right now. The ironic part is that this is kind of like programming because even though a language like C is extremely fast, you still have individuals who prefer things like Python, PHP, and Ruby. Those languages are easier to work with and so they're more preferred even though the language of C is actually faster in a lot of the cases. It's not about the speed of the program itself, it's about whether you can fully break down and understand how the program itself is working. Therefore, many people prefer interpreted languages because it's easier to understand human syntax rather than the many different nuances that come with machine code and bytecode that humans aren't capable of conceiving.

This difference in interpretation normally comes from the issue that we have as humans in that we often describe our surroundings by utilizing objects. We have this directly in our code in the form of object-oriented programming, which allows us to orient the objects in programming or relate programming to objects so as to make it easier for us to program. There have been several different movements to try and get rid of this object-oriented programming methodology but due to the ease of this type of programming, it's very difficult to get rid of. The reason why people have tried to get rid of it before is that there are several very pronounced bugs that naturally come with programming something in a way where the programming doesn't really make sense for the machine but it makes sense for the human.

Machines Vs. Humans

The ironic thing about neural networks is that we're also basing it off of a very buggy program. Human minds are actually littered with bugs and it only takes a minor delving into psychology to see this. The human mind is built to recognize patterns by default and this means that we will find patterns even in the most ridiculous of things. A good example of this is to put two apples about two inches apart and then a banana underneath it. What you will recognize is either a frowny face or a smiling face. This is absolutely ludicrous due to the fact that it's just two apples and a banana, but we're so tuned to recognizing patterns that we see a face when there is no actual face. This becomes a problem with neural networks due to the fact that they do not know how to recognize faces right off of the bat. Therefore, one of the most common beginner neural networks that was created when they were first starting out was one that could recognize faces and this was done by Facebook. Facebook was able to make a neural network tell the difference between edges and then begin to piece together an actual human face based off of those edges and if the human face met a certain set of parameters, it would auto-identify that as a face. The problem with this is that it takes in several different assumptions about what a face looks like. For instance, the parameters could be that it has a triangle in the middle with two ovals on either side that are raised above the triangle with an elliptical shape down below the triangle. The reason why this is a problem is that not everyone has a nose, not everyone has both eyes, and on a very rare occasion, some people do not have the standard mouth that you expect to see. This created several different issues with this type of neural network but because of our parameters, we begin to see how the human mind has a specific bias when it comes to recognizing faces. We understand that those biases will interfere with how a neural network should learn how to recognize a face but some of these biases are almost impossible to fix. Therefore, when creating a neural network you also have to deal with the bugs that are inside of the human neural network.

19

ARTIFICIAL NEURAL NETWORK

Neurons

The primary component in an artificial neural network, the point of this book, is the actual neuron itself. The neuron is a decision tree that ultimately decides the next PATH for the data to go through. For instance, let's say that the neuron has a Boolean value of false. This would mean that the neuron would send the information to point J, which will further decide, based on a Boolean value, where it's going to send the next information. To do this, you not only have to have a decision tree inside of the neuron itself but also some weights and biases otherwise known as Pathways and biases. Let's talk about the decision tree just so that you understand a little bit more about it. The decision tree is where your bulk code is going to go because it ultimately decides what the neural network is going to decide. Normally, such an area is vastly complex and has had months of work going into this because you don't normally create a neural network by yourself. There is a reason why there are teams of people working on neural networks (such as Tensor made by Google). While implementing a neural network is extremely simplistic in some cases, depending on what you choose it can be really complex. A great example of a decision tree is if you are trying to find out if something looks like a face or not from a black and white photo. If there is more white than black inside of a photo, then you would say that you have found a contrast in the color. Based on the bias of the current node known as a neuron, you would determine that this area would need to be explored more. Thus, it would go to a more important node or neuron by utilizing a heavier weight in the neuron tree. If it was important at that point that the color was darker than the remainder of the colors then it would finally output that it found a darker color at that point. By collectively finding the darkest parts of a photo, you would essentially be able to find the outlines of a photo and thus be able to identify things like faces, trees, and other such objects. This is a very basic example of how to utilize a decision tree to find out if there is a face in a picture or not and it is only a partial representation of how Neural Networks are actually working today.

Weights

As we've mentioned before, weights are the pathways in which the neural network travels. There are some Pathways that are more important than others and so we put something called weights on them, which really just means that that pathway has a bigger integer than the other pathways or that the pathway has a smaller integer than other pathways. The bigger or smaller is really depending on how the neural network is developed. However, essentially, you are figuring out which paths are the more important pathways to travel so that information that is seen as important by the neural network travels down the more important pathways so that it ends up competing with more important information or becoming the output at the end. In most neural networks, the act of changing the weights is actually how the machine learns and how you train it. Essentially, during training, you figure out where the best paths are making the right choices so that you can lower the weights of those making the wrong choices. By fine-tuning the weights, you effectively make the machine recognize where the correct paths are much better than it had in the previous training sessions.

Bias

Another part that controls how the information travels through the network is the bias set by the neurons itself. For example, going back to the black and white photo, we can say that certain neurons set to look at the center of the picture are more important than the neurons that are set to look at the outside of a picture. By doing this, we are saying that the neurons have a heavier bias to the center neurons than the outer neurons. This is not how all biases work, but this is a good example of how a bias really should work because these biases allow them to judge whether an area that the neural network is working on needs a higher priority. The reason why we chose the center of a photograph is due to the fact that many people prefer to be the center shot in a photograph unless they are with other people.

Input and Output

The most crucial part of any neural network is what you put into it and what you get out of it. This is represented by the input and output, which is just like any other program that you put into a machine and that has been developed over time. The only difference is that machines work with numbers and you can't really tell a machine that something looks black but, rather, you can provide it the hexadecimal number of #000000 and the Machine will process this as being the color black. This means that whenever you're dealing with things like contrast where you're trying to tell whether something is darker or brighter, you have to deal with numbers such as those found in HEX color or, ultimately, RGB or red, green and blue. The computer works off of a combination of 255 different variations of red, green, and blue with individual variations for each of them. Therefore, if you decide to say that the area is completely devoid of any color, otherwise known as black, you would see the RGB representation of this as RGB (0,0,0). Since the computer has no issue in finding colors that match a certain palette since it has to color those pictures in the first place, it will be able to easily tell whether a specific pixel is black or not. Even better, you could have a system that has a neural network studying sections and in which case you would have a bias if there is more black than white in a specific area but not all black. By saying something is all black, you are essentially saying that there is nothing there but black. Instead, such as in our face photo, you would want to find a varying shade of black that represents an outline. All information going into a neural network has to be represented by either string characters or numeric values. Let's talk about the more meta part of this. In reality, you have one set of inputs and possibly thousand sets of outputs. You see, the output that you get at the very end of the neural network is the network output that you see. However, as we've already discussed, every neuron will produce a result that is ultimately sent out to a different neuron. The only difference is that by the time it reaches the output that you see, the final decision has been made at that point but when the neural network is passing the information along biases and weights you don't see that information. We'll talk about this a little bit more when we get to the different layers of a neural network.

Classifications and Classifiers

Whenever a specific neuron decides what a specific thing is, it has made a classification. Depending on the size of a neural network, it could make tens to hundreds to even thousands of different classifications in the process of ultimately providing you with an output. We've already talked about what goes into these specific neurons but the method of classification is often determined by the classifier. As we've talked about in previous chapters, neural networks are not general-purpose tools and they have to be geared towards a specific task for now. They can't really do anything too complicated when it comes to everyday life. But they do have some wonderful applications with the extreme dedication that they can provide. Whenever we talk about classifiers, we are basically talking about the method of choosing how to classify some of the information. Essentially, a classifier is really just the name of the methodology of classification. Thus, whenever you go searching for different types of neural networks, you have to actually search for classifiers. We will go over different deep learning methodologies in a separate chapter, but let's make a clear distinction here. You can either have a classification or a recognized pattern. When we talk about classifications, we are actually talking about object classifications. This is different from numerical pattern recognition. Numerical pattern recognition is represented with graphs and data that only relates to numerical values. If we're talking about something like the color of an object or the object itself, we are talking about a classification. If we are taking properties and utilizing those properties to make an object out of them then it becomes a classification but if we're taking numerical values and providing numerical values based on patterns, we are talking about pattern recognition. There is a significant difference between the two individual forms since they provide you with different information.

Vanishing Gradient

Vanishing gradient refers to an obvious yet abstract pattern that occurs within a neural network. As you already know, neurons base their information on what the previous neuron gave it. This can happen with forward propagation and backwards propagation, which we will discuss in a later section. Essentially, as the information travels to neurons, the amount of information that travels to a specific neuron grows more complicated as it goes forwards or backwards. The Vanishing gradient refers to the fact that if something is exponentially complex, the time to make a decision on that data becomes exponentially high. For a very long time, deep belief networks and the majority of neural networks were extremely difficult to train in complex situations due to the vanishing gradient, which refers to how time can grow exponentially with complexity.

Layers: Input, Hidden, and Output

There are three layers when it comes to a neural network and the reason why I have a section on input and output and then also a section on layers is that most people who deal with neural networks refer to them as layers rather than input and output. The input layer is where the user is putting in the necessary information into the neural network. This could be any number of different data sets that they're providing, but the idea is that this is the layer in which the individual is inputting information and it may not even be on a code level. You see, when we talk about the input layer we could actually be talking about a graphical user interface that the individual is using in order to put the input into the system. This would mean that the team of developers have created a neural network for non-developers to use. This is why it's really referred to as the layer of inputs because not only could there be a vast difference in the inputs themselves but also a vast difference in the users of such technology. This is also why the output is actually called an output layer because not only could you be dealing with numbers coming from a command line but you could also be rendering it to HTML so that they could see it in the browser or into the Windows' box so that they can see it on software. Essentially, calling it layers is much easier because then you can cover the vast differences in users and the variables that are sent out. After all, a programmer will be able to understand what RGB is but that doesn't really mean anything for the average user. Now, we've already hit on this before but whenever the neural network is working on the information, the network is sending out tens to hundreds to even thousands of different outputs but only the end result is what the user sees. This area, because you don't actually see it, is called the hidden layer and so whenever people are working on neural networks they refer to this area as the hidden layer not only because when someone else decides to use a neural network library they will likely not be looking inside the neural network to see how it works but also because you don't actually see any of the decisions being made by the neural network until the neural network is finished with all the decisions that it makes, which produces the final output.

Forward Propagation and Backward Propagation

A lot of people like to talk about these two topics separately but I have no idea why since they're so simple to understand. Forward propagation is what happens whenever you are putting in inputs and those inputs get to the output. This means that you are propagating the information forward. Likewise, when you are performing a backward propagation, you are taking the outputs that you figured out and going through the reverse process so that you can see what's going on in the system or to produce different inputs to see if you are getting the correct pathways you intended.

GPU Training

For a long time, the CPU was the main component that was utilized in training neural networks but the problem with CPUs is that there aren't enough cores to do anything truly complex. For instance, the most number of cores that a CPU has is around 32 to 64 cores, which are inside of server processors. Server processors are rather expensive. Therefore, some brilliant individual decided to change from using CPU cores to using GPU cores. Since the amount of GPU cores there are has skyrocketed over the years, one has access to not 32 cores but almost two thousand and more cores inside of a GPU. This can easily shrink years of training into days. Therefore, if you are going to play around with neural networks, I highly suggest that you get a really good graphics card so that you have plenty of cores to play around with.

KERAS MODEL AND LAYERS

Keras is one of the easiest forms of neural networking that you can start out with when you're just beginning your adventure on learning how neural networks works and how to implement them on your own. However, you will have to do a lot of research beforehand before you're able to effectively use this API. Additionally, I highly suggest that if you don't know Python that you go to some website and learn it or you can use this to translate what you already know in other programming languages to Python.

What is Keras?

If you are familiar with programming languages that are also interpreted programming languages then you will understand what I'm talking about when I say that Keras is an interpreted form of neural networking. The design principle behind this API is to make neural networking much easier to implement and much faster to scale. The beautiful thing about this API is that it not only shortens the amount of work that you need to do in order to get a fully functioning neural network in your hands but it also runs on top of pre-existing architecture like Theano and TensorFlow. Probably the best part about this API is that it is written in Python, which shows just how far the developing team wanted to make the API user-friendly. Python is a very easy programming language to pick up and it's one of the recommended starter languages for people to learn about programming. You have to import the API into your file and then you can begin creating the model using the different layers of the API to create your neural network. This API works solely on models and layers so it's very important that you understand the difference between the two and how they relate to each other. You can find Keras here.

What is a Keras Model?

Models are how you begin inside of this API and there are two specific models when talking about the different models that this API has. There is the Sequential model and then there's the Model functional model. The Sequential model is a play on words, kind of like the actual name of the API itself, in that it runs everything sequentially. You can think of the model as the easy mode when it comes to handling this API and it is one of the very first models that you utilize in order to begin to understand how to work with this API. On the other hand, you have the Model model. Once you get a thorough understanding of the Sequential model, you can then move on to the more advanced model. This model allows you to fully customize how you want things to be carried out and that doesn't necessarily mean that you're going to want your actions to be carried out in sequential order. However, that doesn't really tell you what a model is.

Inside of this API, the Model Class is how you utilize the different aspects of the neural network. This means that if you are trying to create a neural network, you first have to set up your model so that you can sequentially or non-sequentially layout the necessary weights, biases, and even the information. Likewise, you can have models interacting with other models to create a more complicated model. Each model represents a separated neural network and so by utilizing your model to interact with other models, you can create a deep neural network. That isn't to say that you can't create one inside of a singular model, but for the purposes of keeping track of everything it's usually good to modulate all the different responsibilities that you want a neural network to do and so that is why you are given the capability of calling on different models to do different things in order to get a completely different output. Now that we understand that the model basically represents a neural network, you now need to understand that each neural network has many and, I do mean, many different layers.

What is a Keras Layer?

Layers represent the different components of a neural network such as the density or the input of a neural network. They are the primary code that you're going to deal with inside of the API and so you need to understand that the list of different layers that there are is not really exhaustive. If you decide to forgo the Sequential model, you can develop your own layers inside of the program so as to do specific things that you want to do such as much more complicated tasks than what is already set inside of the program but this is kind of rare. They leave it open just in case you're one of those developers who's working on a massively complex system that requires a lot of customization. If you're trying to utilize models or layers, you're going to have to import everything that you want to utilize. Again, this API doesn't assume that you need everything that they've created and so you cannot simply import a model and gain access to the enormous API that they've created. This allows you to have code that runs smoothly and efficiently while also being user-friendly. Additionally, as you can use other models with a singular model, you can also utilize multiple layers with multiple inputs.

What do you need to understand going into Keras?

The developers of this API assume that you understand how neural networking works in the first place and if you don't understand how neural networking works, I suggest you read the rest of the book and do a little further delving into the technology before you go about using this API. The reason why I suggest this is because it makes it so easy to implement a neural network that it clouds a lot of the technical definitions behind what you're implementing. Therefore, if you don't know what RELU is then you're out of luck because this API assumes you already know that and if you want to implement it, you have to learn about what that is before you can apply it to the neural network properly.

Like a Good Nerd, Classical Literature References Are There For You

This is just a side note but the developers who decided to give us access to this API also have a deep love for Greek literature, specifically The Odyssey. The actual name of this API comes from the Odyssey where there is a tale of a horn gate and an ivory gate, which represents the horn gate as being the true gate to go through while the ivory gate is one of deceit. Whenever available, the developers of this group will often name important things in this API after the Greek literature.

DEEP LEARNING ALGORITHMS

RBM: Restricted Boltzmann Machine

The most prominent of all machine learning algorithms is RBM because it gave us the biggest breakthrough for developing neural networks by dealing with the vanishing gradient. Essentially, you have an input layer and a hidden layer with the input layer being the output layer. The hidden layer is only made up of a single set of neurons, which minimizes the amount of propagation. The important part here is that none of the nodes in the hidden layer share a connection to other nodes in the hidden layer. Training an RBM is a quick process due to these restrictions. The input is first sent to the hidden layer so that it can be transformed. After the data has been changed, a replacement of weights and/or biases is provided whether it be the same or different weights and/or biases. It is then sent back to the input layer, which has now become the output layer, to provide a reconstruction of that data. If the information is wrong, the weights and/or biases are adjusted until the reconstruction of the data is correct. RBM is part of the family known as Autoencoders and it works wonderfully with unlabeled data.

DBN: Deep Belief Network

As you can tell, from the last Deep Learning Algorithm, we haven't explained how an RBM helped solve the vanishing gradient issue, which is where DBN comes in. DBN is a combination of RBM's that have been put together on the same job but working on different tasks. DBNs are similar to MLPs in their structure, but they are completely the opposite when it actually comes down to training the neural network and that has to do with their implementation. Essentially, with a DBN you have RBM's interconnected by making each hidden layer the input layer in succession. Therefore, let's go over this in four steps. In step one, we add an input into the input layer. In step two, that input goes through its first RBM to become changed output. In step three, that hidden layer becomes the new input layer for the next RBM. This cycle repeats until it gets to the end. With each layer of RBM, the classifications are handling different parameters of the feature that require less and less abstraction of the data.

CNN: Convolutional Neural Networks

Convolutional neural networks are pretty much where most of the neural networking world is focused on. The reason being is because it is the forefront or the most newly discovered version of neural networking and it has a lot of applications. It has a lot of applications due to the fact that it can take unlabeled data, as the previous two did, and organize it into labeled data even if the data is changed slightly. Convolutional Networks actually work by utilizing two different Mathematical solutions. The first mathematical solution is filtering and filtering means that you use a mathematical equation to filter your results, such as finding the edges inside of a picture. Essentially, if an edge has a black color then you give it a 1, if it has a gray color then you give it at 0, and if it has a white color then you give it -1. A good example of a good filter would be multiplying every pixel value by the pixel value next to it. Whenever the pixels are black and black, you will always get a 1 and if they are white then you will get a 1. However, if you multiply 0 by -1 you get 0 and if you multiply 0 by 1 you get 0. This will tell the network that there is a difference in color there and so it will put that value there. The next mathematical solution comes from convolutional mathematics, which is to say that you are going to try all the different values over and over until you get to the end of trying all the values. The last part of the convolutional network is the filtering itself, which is to say that the data is then sectioned off into features so that it can examine specific blocks of the code. For instance, say you have a 40 x 40 grid of pixels. You would then use filtering to only go over every 10x10 pixels or 4x4 pixels to do your filtering. You use convolutional mathematics to try each of these filtered areas so as to provide a representative value of those areas: The center of each window of pixels, whatever size you choose, is then added up with each of the pixel values and divided by the number of pixels in the window size you choose. Therefore, if you choose a window of four pixels then it would be:

$$(a + b + c + d)/4$$

The final step in this convolutional process is to actually start at different locations inside of whatever you're looking at. Therefore, if you decided to start up at the left-hand corner and multiply everything on the right-hand side, then you would start at the right-hand corner and multiply by everything on the left side. You would do this for each of the possible directions that you have and then you would have several different images that have different numbers representing whatever you're looking at. These several different images represent the convolutional layer.

We're still not done though because this only represents the convolutional layer of the convolutional neural network. There are two more steps that are commonly used in convolutional neural networks, but they simply reduce the workload of the neural network themselves. This is where it's going to get confusing because we're going to do something called pooling. Pooling is the act of taking a specific size window, such as a 2x2 or a 4x4 pixel window and then selecting 2 or 4 pixels in which to move (known as a Stride) and going over each window of pixels in that image. Then you take the maximum values that you can obtain from each of those windows. If you get to a section that doesn't have a complete window, you are still just going to take the maximum value. This can shrink the array down by nearly half, a third, or even a fourth of the original size. This is the section of a CNN that handles indiscriminate changes in an object or an image due to the fact that it's still only going to take the maximum value. The last step in the changing process is to normalize the data or, rather, turn it all back to integers rather than doubles or floats and this just means you take all the negatives and put them as a null or a zero, otherwise known as RELU (Rectified Linear Units). All of this is then Deep Stacked, which is to say these final outputs become the new inputs until you get a tiny dataset at the end. Each of the values in the tiny set gets a judgment that serves as a prediction of whether something is one thing, another thing, or nothing. These are known as Votes and whoever gets the most of these will be the prediction. This guess is then you decide whether the network made an error or not. If it is wrong, the weights are changed where the network first went down the path of errors.

By doing this, you can take normal shapes that are a little bit wonky and still get a similar result even if they aren't exactly alike. For instance, if you took a car photo and applied a liquefying feature on it, the convolutional network would still end up with the same values, but they would be in slightly different places and so the convolutional network would still recognize the outline of the object and if it was close enough to match the outline that it already has in the neural network then it would be able to identify that object as the object you're trying to find. This makes convolutional neural networks absolutely vital when it comes to machine learning because it can take distorted data and recognize the patterns inside of it whereas a normal neural network would not be able to do this. The problem is that CNNs need to be supervised, which means that data needs to be collected and supplied to the CNN. This is a huge problem, especially when you think of it in terms of identifying faces. A good example of this problem is that Apple just recently got in trouble for claiming that it had trained its facial recognition software by utilizing over one billion faces. The obvious question, asked by a Senator in the U.S., was "Where did you get these?" and this now becomes an explosive privacy issue.

Perceptron: IMPORTANT!!!!

I know that this could have been included in a previous section but I wanted to wait until we got to talking about the different types of algorithms that networks can use because we need to talk about the one that started it all. The Perceptron was the very first and simplest neural network ever created. The best part about the Perceptron was that it was extremely simple to understand. It would take in an immeasurable amount of inputs and always produce either a one or a negative one. This is where you're going to learn how your neuron works. Essentially, imagine you have however many inputs you have going into a singular neuron that is then connected to the output. The output will be your prediction and the inputs will be your data set. Inside of the neuron, you take the sum of the inputs that you're going to give the neuron along with the weights that the inputs are traveling on. You then use a mathematical function to reduce the data that has been given to the neuron to either a one for activation or a negative one for deactivation. This is why this step is called the Activation Function and it is inside of every single neural network neuron. The most common implementation of how to get your +1 or -1 is to use the sine function. So, because this is so important, let's get down into the math. Let's say I have a pocketbook of bills but I don't know if they are dollars or hundreds of dollars. Therefore, I will feed our imaginary machine all of the bills in my pocket and now there is a weight for every single bill I have. Let's say that our weights go from one to ten because I have ten bills. Now, since I have ten bills and I'm trying to figure out how much of each I have, it becomes a different type of solution in the neuron. We'll call this the "how much of each" function. You know that question you asked Google about how much of something is and it presents you with some actual measurements of its own? This is similar to that. Therefore, it takes each of them, one at a time, and counts them. Obviously, we could just set up an algorithm to count each of the bills and we're done, but now I'm going to throw a monkey wrench in there. I want to know how much I keep on hand throughout the year by weeks. Now, instead of the algorithm calculating how much I keep on average, I want it to predict the following year of weekly money I have in my pockets. You might go, "well, that can be solved by finding the average of each month." but I say, "Nay!" Let me show you why.

Let's say that I have a week, randomly according to human standards, where I don't have any money. The algorithm would have been set up to keep track of how much money I had on hand each week for a year. Then the algorithm would have access to all of that data. As of right now, the program gives me a +1 if I will have over $500 and a -1 respectively. It will also do this for $200 and $100. In order to predict what I want it to predict, I need to hand it an equation that would be handled by one neuron. Remember, we're just handling this with one neuron. This equation would have to figure out my average by month, by six-month, by bi-weekly, and by tri-month. It would then need to notice any similarities between the weeks I had nothing and the weeks I had something. We would say our habits are random, but, oh look, I've got no cash money either on a day near the end of the month or near the beginning of the month. For month 1, I had no money on the first week, then no money on the second week of month 2, no money on the third week of month 3, no money on the first week of month 4, no money on the last week of month five, six, and seven, but then I have no money on the second week of month eight, no money in the third week of month 9, no money on the last week of month 10, 11, and 12. Now, most would think that the pattern is the end of the month but that only accounts for some of them. The last thing I'm going to do is give the algorithm access to the calendar and all events will be listed on it. Low and behold, 90%

of the time the algorithm will now tell me I have no money on Holidays and Major Events. New Years, Valentine's, March Madness, April Fool's Day, Graduation Day for most kids, an oddity to the system, Independence Day, Start of School for most kids, a birthday, Halloween, Thanksgiving, and Christmas. As I said, the average person would look for a correlation for the end of the month but the machine would automatically see that there is an event nearly every time I'm broke. What about the rest of the guesses? Not just if I am broke, but the three remaining measurements. How can a single Neuron keep track of money, current date, future dates, previous dates, currency value, and events if it is meant to do something more than run the average mill of a program? It can't without a heavy amount of writing, but what if it could? Let's talk about the MLP.

MLP: Multi-layer Perceptron

Originally, the Perceptron was actually built to detect faces. That's right, in 1957, they were trying to work out technology that would allow them to recognize faces and they failed horribly. However, due to their wonderful experiences, we now have what is known as neural networking and we also now have facial recognition software. What they found out with their first Perceptron was that it didn't give back a lot of good predictions primarily because it couldn't handle all of the different variables and it wasn't good at keeping track of multiple layers of information. Who am I kidding, it was the humans that were the problem and they simply couldn't program the neuron to do multiple layers of calculations that seem unconnected. Instead, they found out that if they used more than one perceptron, they could keep the code simple enough to where they could code what they needed to code and this became the first neural network. The Perceptron was a whole bunch of singularly powered neurons but they each worked on separate jobs, much like our computers do. We simply didn't have the algorithms necessary for them to work interconnectedly. Now, going from a single process to a multi-process is actually pretty easy because all you have to do is figure out how to get them to work on separate jobs so that when they come together they produce a combined result. We do this all the time in programming, it's just a little bit more difficult whenever you're talking about hardware. This is where the MLP or Multi-layer perceptron comes from. They found that with the added amount of Perceptrons, the prediction rates became significantly better.

Recurrent Net

The problem with the deep learning patterns that we've discussed before is that They Don't Really Work Well when you need to change it on the fly. A good example of this, which we have constantly come back to, is language. For instance, the phrase "Netflix and chill" has several different meanings to it and getting a computer to understand the new nuance of Netflix and chill requires that the machine learning process be able to stop and learn what that is. When you're running something like a CNN, you can't really stop the process mid process due to the fact that it is feeding the information for it and there is no way for it to temporarily halt so that you can change the data, which is where Recurrent networks come in handy. However, RNNs are not the best for language, but they can handle language. The best, current method for handling language is RNTN, which we will talk about next. Essentially, you should think of RNNs as networks that change with every set of neurons. Each set of neurons is handed the information from the previous set of neurons along with any set of neurons that may be running at the same time as those neurons. This allows the network to perform much more complex tasks. The difference between the network from the previous ones that we have been discussing is that the network is enclosed. The set of neurons is a single set of neurons rather than input neuron and a decision neuron. Instead, a single set of neurons serves as both an input and a decision maker. This allows each set of neurons to quickly capture information as it moves down the chain without being incapable of stopping midway to reorganize the information. This is why it's really useful for things such as traffic predictions, language predictions, and many other "immediate change" types of data. The problem with this type of network is that it doesn't really know when to forget the information because it's useless. Since we're basically utilizing each second in time as a separate neural network and passing it to the next second in time neural network, we run into the wall of the vanishing gradient. The only way to deal with this is known as gating, which is where we manually select when the network should forget something. There are several methods for gating such as Gradient Clipping, Steeper Gates, LSTM, and GRU. There is no set, defined way of handling the gating process. These types of networks are really only useful if you're trying to deal with regression or forecasting of language rather than classification. This is due to the unique setup of the actual network in that being able to regress an item or forecast an item requires you to be able to control the time flow of data.

RNTN: Recursive Neural Tensor Nets

The complexity around language has to do with the syntactical nature of language itself. This means that in order to predict the words that are coming out of my mouth, Google Voice would have to be able to learn the structure of the syntactical language and this is rather difficult if you're just dealing with strings. Therefore, instead of dealing with just strings they are vectorized. This means that each specific component in a string is given a number to represent its value and the string as well as its likelihood to be connected to certain other words in a dictionary. Once the entire string is completely formed, it chooses one of the different sets of strings that were judged by other methodologies and it compares the highest score of predictable analysis in order to see which is the best string. It must first recognize the different syntactical groupings such as a noun phrase or a verb phrase and give scores to those that make more sense than others. This calculates into the overall final value of the prediction. The recursive part of the neural network comes from the fact that it does this with every single set of words inside of a singular sentence. Therefore, if you had a sentence with only four words in it, this means that it would produce about three different trees due to the fact that you could group the words 3 times. You would have the first two words, the middle 2 words, and the last 2 words in your grouping but, as you can see, it gets rather difficult whenever there are more words in a sentence. Thanks to the thousands or millions or even billions of individuals utilizing Google Voice to do their typing, they're texting, and even their searches, these people have dedicated themselves to the constant learning machine that is Google Voice.

BENEFITS OF NEURAL NETWORKS

A Faster Human Brain

There are several benefits to our creation of neural networks. However, the primary reason why most individuals want to create a fully optimized and fully working neural network is that it's a faster human brain. You see, the brain does several things that machines simply can't do such as be able to speak languages with ever-changing nuances and syntax modifications. A good example of this is the word "own." This word has had a couple different changes throughout history. Over the general course of this words' history, it has come to mean the possession of something and while possessing something is a very simplistic concept, the word itself has had different meanings in the contextual sense. For instance, you can own a building that employs workers but you can also, even though it's really immoral and illegal to do so, own human beings. This is the property form of possession. However, you can also own up to your responsibilities or own up to your feelings, which means that you are emotionally possessing something that you previously were not possessing. This shows that there is a difference between possessing emotions and property. The last type of definition is one of saying that you owned a person after you've defeated them. This is a very unique and rather new version of the word that represents defeat rather than possession. You have three different contextual meanings of the word while also having the same definition for only two of them. If you owned a person, you either possess them as a property or you defeated them and this becomes a problem for regular machines developed by hand that are checking for syntax. If the sentence is talking about how they defeated someone in a game, a machine that has not been developed to take into account the newer definition of the word would be unable to correctly grammatically check that sentence. A neural network that constantly updates itself on the nuances of English would be able to predict this without a programmer having to manually input the language itself. On top of this, the programmer would not need to manually put in all the multitude of nuances, contexts, and grammar changes that affect our daily speech.

Better at Dedicated Tasks

This leads to our next benefit of having a neural network and that would be that they are better at dedicated tasks. A human mind has a lot of things going on whenever it focuses on work, which can actually get in front of the work and prevent them from doing the work. For instance, a human might have children that are constantly distracting them from completing the work, they might also have hardware issues that are completely negating what they're trying to do, and even worse is that they may actually be sick. These are all outside variables that are affecting how the human is actually working and they are uniquely related to human biology. You might be thinking that I stretched it a little bit with "hardware issues" but what I'm talking about is someone at work didn't do their job properly and now there is a slowing of traffic online so that the human is unable to look up web pages, which would affect neural networks that were specifically connected to the internet but since humans would likely be gathering databases and preventing neural networks from having access to the online world due to safety concerns, this makes the issue uniquely human. Additionally, while a neural network could throw all of its processing power at a mathematical problem, a human has to wait for something called creativity. Let's say that we're on the cutting edge of physics and we are trying to solve a problem that no one has ever tackled before. A human would likely break the things down into bite-size chunks and spend nearly a decade or more on solving a problem. There would be several moments where the human managed to overcome the new age mathematics but the problem would be that they didn't know the next step. A neural network would be able to run through thousands of different calculations in order to come up with the necessary mathematical equation that you were dealing with at the time. The reason why the machine would be faster at doing this would simply be due to the fact that the human is only capable of sending one processor at the problem while we could send hundreds of thousands of processors with a machine.

A Further Abstraction of Mathematics

This leads to our next benefit of having a neural network that can be dedicated to a specific task, which is also capable of forming thoughts in a similar manner to a human being, which is to say that we are able to have a further abstraction of mathematics. Mathematics, as an industry, is about as abstract as it gets even when comparing it to some of the stuff that comes out of human artwork. For instance, reading the mathematical equations of quantum physics can often either make someone drool out of anticipation or make someone drool out of a coma. It's not really something that's for everyone but the abstraction level of quantum physics is remarkably high. The thing about it is that humans are not built to think abstractly because we are built to think in a way that allows us to function as the meat suit that we are in. This means that we look at everything from the vantage point of ourselves rather than the things around us. Into the latter end of Mathematics, you come up against thinking so abstractly that you are thinking in the terms of the universe. Essentially, you are trying to put a mathematical equation on the universe and thinking on this level of abstraction is extremely difficult for the human mind, which is why a lot of people can't do it that much. The thing is that we are able to do it but we are not able to do it much. We have several different biases that keep us grounded in an individual perspective and so to ask a human mind to think abstractly, you are asking us to do something that we are biologically built to not do very well. However, since we are able to do it by a little, we have something like mathematics in our world and we have been better because of it. A machine, on the other hand, doesn't have this limitation due to the fact that it doesn't think of items in terms of itself. You have to conceptualize the fact that a neural network is just a whole bunch of light switches that are specifically placed to do certain things that will ultimately change how those light switches are placed over time. This means that if you give a neural network the ability to solve mathematical equations and develop it to increase the complexity of the mathematical equations that it is meant to solve, you inevitably end up with an entire library of mathematical equations that max out their complexity. Unless you introduce a new variable into the equation, it will only create mathematical equations based off of the rules that you give it. If your rules are abstract and can mean many different things then the results of the equations that you're looking for are going to be abstract in it of themselves. The problem is that we haven't gotten to that point and there are many people who are afraid that if we hand over the mathematics to the neural networks when it is capable of doing such a thing, it will eventually create a complexity that is so high that humans can't understand it and that the singularity will happen. The honest truth is that none of us really know what could happen if we make a neural network too complex for our own understanding. However, given a controlled set of mathematical equations, we can give the neural networks something to solve that would take us hundreds even thousands and millions of years to solve on our own. This includes simulations of how the universe would work. We are not at an advanced level enough that would allow us to hand over our more complicated and abstract works of mathematics so that the neural networks could create new fields of mathematics for us. However, we are coming to that point and this means that we will have new fields of mathematics that are generated by machines that will propel us forward in society extremely fast due to the fact that we use those mathematics to create the tools and technology that we use in society.

Better Threat Detection

A Neural network is usually designed so that it can predict something or collect an analysis on something. One of the better use cases for a neural network is threat detection itself. As of right now, threat detection is a little bit outside of the scope of neural networks but it does hold some promise. The reason why neural networks are little bit out of the scope right now is actually due to humanity's inability to control their biases. The human body or rather the human mind is built to be biased against others that are foreign to the community. Humans are, normally, a social creature that prefers to stay within tightly-knit communities and anything outside of the community is usually seen as a threat. This is part of the reason why it's very difficult to go up to strangers and just start talking to them because you feel that sense of danger whenever you go up to something you don't know and you attempt to converse with it. This strangeness shows itself in some very ugly ways such as racism, elitism, and even ageism. These natural biases prevent us from being able to truly predict who is threatening and who is not but some pseudoscience could help in this realm due to the fact that humans are capable of detecting liars. Well, that's not entirely humanly true, it's that we've created machines that can give you a high probability of whether a human is lying or not. This includes many things from stressing in the voice, body language, and several other different factors but the same can actually be true of those who pose a threat. For instance, a suicide bomber that's brand new would likely show signs of being nervous and anxious when they're about to do what they are about to do. Anyone that's in a gang that's not supposed to be doing what they are currently doing will show signs of being stressed, anxious, and an increased level of hormones. Technically speaking, we could build machines that take the psychological aspects of the human mind, the different chemicals that make up the human body, the specific chemicals that run through an individual that is going to do something that they know is wrong or that will likely bring danger to their life, and combine this into a predictive analysis of whether an individual is threatening the lives of others. The problem is that this is extremely invasive and we build things based on what we know, which means that if you are particularly partial towards a specific race or a specific gender than these detection methods would be affected by how you think a threatening individual should be detected. Not only that, there is a very famous example of a machine learning to be biased against a certain race thanks to Google because they found out that the Google search engine was more racist to black individuals due to a number of times that black individuals came under a need for a background search. Due to the heavy increase, they found that you were more likely to be suggested for background searches when you searched for black individuals then you would any other individuals. Therefore, anything that we put into the system relies on the biases that we have at the time and the biases that happen at the end of the system because neural networks are built with the knowledge that you don't normally know what the end is going to be in a real-world scenario.

BUSINESS APPLICATIONS OF NEURAL NETWORKS

Removing the Need for Mundane Tasks

The first and most obvious of all the different business applications that neural networks could provide is the removal of mundane tasks. A good example of how we've used machines to remove a giant portion of mundane tasks are the assembly lines for most of the more advanced companies in the world that provide products. You have packaging machines, weight machines, quality assurance machines, and the list honestly just is not exhaustive anymore. However, you do have a few mundane tasks that are still performed by humans. The first and most obvious of them is filing because there are individuals who are hired simply to file away papers. For instance, a bookkeeper is required to file away a lot of papers during their work unless their company is online or software-based. Even then, a bookkeeper usually has to file something away because most people don't just trust their software. After all, what happens to the information if the software is on a computer that blows

64

up. Honestly, this could be easily solved by training a neural network to file papers away in the proper order. Many different businesses have many different ways of filing, but a neural network would be able to learn how the files are filed away so that instead of the bookkeeper spending nearly a quarter of her or his time filing paperwork the bookkeeper just places a stack of papers on a rack that is controlled by a neural network. The neural network would then be able to utilize the machines given to it to file away papers in the proper order according to the business. This would save the bookkeeper time so that if the business was one where the bookkeeper had to handle hundreds of customers, they wouldn't have to worry about filing away the papers and wasting time on that mundane task. This is just one exclusive example of how neural networks could save the employee's time so that they could work more proficiently. Another example is the ever-useless phone fix shops that are found practically everywhere. As an individual who has fixed many phones before, I can tell you that if you fixed one iPhone you've pretty much fixed almost all of them. The sad truth is that many iPhones are built exactly the same in terms of component placement. Even worse, Android phones are usually such a difficult fix that the price for fixing it is usually worth more than the phone. Therefore, unless you're needing something very specific off of the phone, which can usually be done by utilizing other tools, you don't normally fix an Android phone screen. This is why I say the phone fix shops are useless because unless you have an iPhone, there isn't much profit to be made inside of a phone fix shop unless you're talking about secondary services such as fixing computers and other types of machines. You could, technically, build a neural network that could handle replacing screens on phones. This would kill nearly half the market when it comes to phone fixing. On the other hand, there can be multiple things wrong with a phone so it doesn't completely kill the market but it does remove the unnecessary mundane task of replacing an LCD screen on a phone. This could also go inside of a phone fix shop and anyone that didn't really know about how technology is fixed would be able to get their phone fixed in much the same way. I say that neural networking would be beneficial when it came to replace something like an entire screen but it wouldn't replace the necessity of technicians. For instance, the issue on an iPhone screen could be caused by some bad components inside of the iPhone itself rather than the iPhone screen. In this instance, repairing the iPhone would require more experience than could be given to a neural network at this time when comparing it to fixing an iPhone screen by replacing the entire screen. It would require knowledge about how electricity works, how to diagnose problems, how to find your way to the problem, and how to actually desolder the old part off and solder the new part on. That's a lot more complex than taking out a couple of screws and replacing a screen. Essentially, it takes out the less critical thinking jobs but eventually, given enough time, you could technically train neural networks to do the same thing as a technician. This is one of the scary factors when it comes to neural networks and the potential that many people see in it.

Effective Advertising

Even advertisers hate advertisements, but you can't really get in the marketing place without advertising that you have services. Therefore, finding effective ways to advertise to people is one of the crucial parts that neural networking can provide. We all know the annoying commercials that pop up in front of our YouTube videos or regular cable television, if you still have that for some reason, and they get really annoying. On the other hand, we also know those commercials that have that bit of comedy that we don't mind missing out on our show for because the commercial itself is hilarious. As we have seen, commercials that don't annoy us actually tend to do a lot better whenever advertising their services. I would have to say one of the only ways that an annoying commercial can really make any progress is to be as annoying as possible. A perfect example of this is the Kia radio commercial that always ends in "it's going to be huge." This has been said so much that it is burned into my brain and has become useful in ending some of my jokes. This is because I heard this commercial so much that I simply couldn't remove it from my mind and that is really the only way an annoying commercial can effectively stick itself in somebody's head. However, Mountain Dew is something that I remember for the funky monkey that showed on television and I found it so bizarre and funny that it has stuck in my head. I only saw that commercial once and it has left a permanent impact on me. As you can see, comedy and weirdness stick better than blasting me with advertisement after advertisement. However, how exactly do you make car insurance funny or how do you make law defense funny? The thing about neural networking is that it is built on pre-designed parameters that people set and so if you teach neural networking comedy or how to learn comedy, you will get a neural networking system that is capable of producing comedy. This would allow such a neural networking machine to provide more effective advertisements or more effective advertisement suggestions to the marketing team that develops the advertisements. Instead of wondering about whether your commercial will be successful or not, you can put in the numbers of how many individuals have watched your previous commercials and the different concepts that went into those commercials, which will give you a prediction from the neural network about whether your commercial idea is going to be successful or not. This would save companies thousands to millions of dollars when it comes to advertising to millions and billions of people. As you can see, such a neural network would have a huge impact on business. Additionally, we would get better commercials.

A Very Precise Prediction Ability

Remember that most of neural networking is centered around making machines think like a human so that it can do human tasks. This means that it is able to think like a human and therefore predict human actions. That doesn't mean that it's perfect in its predictions, it just means that it can give you a percentage of how much something is likely to happen. This is due to the probability analysis that occurs whenever you map out the commonality of certain actions. A great example is if an individual is likely to eat a chocolate bar on Sunday when he eats or she eats a chocolate bar every day of the week. You can expect the confidence level of the neural network to say that they are 99.9% repeating confident that the human is going to eat a chocolate bar. On the other hand, if the human eats a chocolate bar 3 times throughout the week then the neural network will likely predict that the odds of the human eating a chocolate bar is dependent on which days he ate the chocolate bar along with the amount of times he ate the chocolate bar. What I mean is, if you have the human eating a chocolate bar Monday, Tuesday, and Wednesday, then it would follow that there is a lower chance of the human eating a chocolate bar on Sunday due to the long strain of the human not eating chocolate bars up until the day of prediction. On the other hand, if the human were to eat a chocolate bar on Monday, on Wednesday, and then finally on Friday, then the odds of the neural network saying that the human is going to eat a chocolate bar on Sunday goes up. This is due to the fact that you can recognize the pattern of the human eating the chocolate bar every other day so since Sunday would technically be an "other" day, we would likely predict that Sunday would be a day where the chocolate was eaten. This not only calculates the probability of how often the human eats the chocolate bar but also in what order the human will eat the chocolate bar. If you complicate things by including the hours at which the human eats the chocolate bar then you also will have a prediction level of the exact hour or range of the hours that the human will eat the chocolate bar. This can be extrapolated to represent models of what humans are likely to do in certain circumstances based on past decisions that they made during those types of circumstances. This is something that a human can easily do on their own until the number of variables becomes too complex for a human to control. For example, in the recent hurricane, everyone rushed the I-75 road, which led to the fact that many individuals were incapable of evacuating due to the sheer volume of individuals on that road. This was not something that many people planned for and so thousands of individuals were left stranded on the road. They didn't have enough gas to make it all the way through I-75. Now, if you take the population that encompasses Florida, you can easily calculate the likelihood that you will have traffic congestion based on the length of the road itself and the number of cars along with their lengths to determine how many cars can fit on a road maximally before you get traffic congestion. However, you will not be able to detect just how many of those people had iPhones with battery packs. I know that that kind of came out of left field so to say, but the truth is that there were so many variables that go into predicting how many people have battery packs and how many people have iPhones on I-75 that trying to predict such a thing during an emergency would be almost ludicrous for human being. As for whether it has a purpose or not, it's not very clear as to why you would want to know why individuals might have an iPhone with battery backups. The point of the situation is that, as a human, this would be so complex that you wouldn't be able to get a very accurate answer. On the other hand, the neural network would probably be able to give you a much better prediction than a human would be able to simply due to the fact that it would be able to calculate for several thousand different variables that you handed it. A human could do the calculations by the way, but they would need far more time since they would need to account for foreigners who owned iPhones, every iPhone that ever existed, every battery pack that ever existed, and how many illegal iPhones might be circulating the state plus more variables I may not be accounting for.

CONCLUSION

Welcome to the end of this book and while this may be the end of the book, you are probably wondering whether there's more to learn about neural networking. Honestly, not really. I really hate to do this to you because normally I say that there is a large path ahead of you with tons of knowledge that you can just suck up but the honest truth is that we covered most of everything. The only thing that we didn't cover is how to actually do it and that can really depend on what you're using. For instance, we provided you with an excellent API that will help you get your feet wet with neural networking but that's only one of probably a hundred different types of API that are out there on the market. Python is just one of many of the languages out there and there are many languages where people have created APIs to handle neural networking from what they considered to be a great programming aspect. For instance, you have Java, C, and C# to begin with. Just these three languages would likely have around 5 to 10 different types of applications where you could employ a neural network. You might be thinking that there might be more complex neural networks out there but the truth of the matter is that neural networking is a pretty new topic and that's kind of why it's all of the rage in the news. It's not really that complicated of a topic, but because of how mystified it is and how giant corporations are in the business, people think that it's a lot more complicated than it really is. This effect is magnified whenever people try to describe it in mathematical terms. From a mathematical standpoint, it is kind of complicated but it's only complicated up until maybe the end of Algebra 2 in terms of understanding how it works. Now, that doesn't mean that you can't get seriously complex with it because it really depends on what you want to do with it. For instance, if you are trying to extrapolate a 3D model from a 2D image then you're going to need some heavy mathematics behind it along with some predictive analysis and some database entries to the shapes of whatever you're trying to extrapolate a 3D model from. It can be as complicated as you want but the technology itself is pretty simple when you begin to understand it. We've actually covered how these things work several different times and the problem with this type of topic is that since you expected this to be a whole new field of technology, you also likely expected it to be far more complicated than it really is. If you understand how the neuron works, you understand how neural networks are connected to each other. What you don't understand at this point is the application of it such as the actual code of the programs that you might want to build off of it or where it can it be applied and this also includes how it can be applied. Basically, you've learned the tool but you haven't learned how to effectively utilize the tool and the only way that can be taught is if you go into a database and start playing around with it. Therefore, I will say my goodbyes and good luck to you on your adventures down the neural networking path.